Finding

Family & Ancestors

Finding

Family & Ancestors

TRACE YOUR ROOTS, LEARN YOUR HISTORY,
KNOW YOUR FAMILY STORY

To: Elidia
Seek your Ancestors
and they guide you!
♡ +x
ATlalli

Alejandra Chikauak-Yaotl Tlalli-Miles

COPYRIGHT PAGE:

For more information, email: findingfamiliaandancestors@gmail.com

ISBN: 979-8-9871529-5-9

INTRODUCTION

The story of my family will be narrated by the information found in the various historical documents that were located. This information offers a snapshot into the lives of my ancestors and establishes kinship. Contained within the documents, we learn of a history that includes teenage pregnancies, infant mortality, racism, intentional erasure of Indigenous identity, political opposition, sickness, and survival. On a universal level, our story speaks to the human experience of love, struggle, celebration, and life. I invite you to join me on this journey and follow the history of a family with deep roots in Michoacán, México. Concluding with photos and a listing of the descendants of the Fernández Barragán family.

This book is organized into four sections. The first section is the story of my grandmother, Angelita (Sahara) Barragán. The second section is about my grandfather, Máximo Fernández. The third section tells the story of my grandparents together, including their family and descendants. In sections 1-3, you will find visual charts, chronicles, and translations of the information that was located in the historical documents. The information is organized to start with the earliest ancestor that I was able to locate.

In the last section, you will find instructions, resources, and a template to help you start your own family/genealogy search and learn your history, and know your family's story.

HOW TO READ THIS BOOK

As I mentioned earlier, this book contains visual charts and narrations of the historical documents that were found. The charts serve to assist the reader to visualize the order of relationships between family members (parent, child, marriage, etc.) and to establish kinship. Each person in the visual chart is listed by a number. That number coincides with the number of the explanation of their historical document. The historical documents that were located include registrations of births, baptisms, intent to marry, marriages, the 1930 census, and registrations of deaths. These documents serve as examples of the different types of documents and the different formats by which municipalities and churches documented events. Also, keep in mind that the persons documenting the events were persons that represented the Catholic church or were employees of the local municipal government. In the oldest documents, there are examples of older Spanish words and terms that probably originate in Spain and are not very common today. When reviewing and reading older documents, it is important to read the documents in their entirety because within the documents there are clues regarding race, identity, age, names of parents, grandparents (both maternal and paternal), places or towns of origin, etc.

The fourth section contains a template to get you started on your family search. Including terms and observations that were a common theme in my findings. Referencing the terminology contained within my family's documents will serve to help you discover additional information as you begin your family search.

ACKNOWLEDGMENTS

This book would not be possible without the ancestors who have guided me to this moment, those whom I was able to locate, and those that remain nameless, faceless, and tribeless, thank you for the guidance. I feel your presence with me. I am grateful for the elders in my family, those that I was able to meet and know my current family members, and our descendants.

I am extremely grateful to my two sons, Kairese and Nakai, for all your love, encouragement, and support with this book and all my personal goals. You both know you are my heart. Thank you, Terrence, my partner, for your love and support. I recognize that it is not easy living with me.

I would like to recognize my sister, Monica, for all your help, support, and unconditional love- I love you sister! To my mom, Angelita, thank you for sharing family stories and listening to all my discoveries and theories, I realize that this has not been easy for you. To my beloved uncle Jesús, thank you for openly sharing family stories.

Many thanks to all my cousins and family members for your words of encouragement and support...I appreciate you very much! Additionally, I would like to thank all my friends for your words of encouragement and your friendship.

A special thank you to my colleague, Jacklyn, for planting the seed that sprouted to move past a family project to this published book. I would also like to thank Mr. John Schmal for responding to my numerous emails and allowing me to use a slide from his presentation and cite his website as a resource. To Native Land Digital- thank you for all your work to further awareness and conversations regarding the history of native territories and Family Search for allowing me to mention them as a resource.

Thank you ~

This book is dedicated to Kairese, Nakai, Ayla, Déjá, Kaya, and Zulu

SPECIAL DEDICATION

Máximo Fernández
1949-2022

Thank you, uncle Max, for all your support with this book and your willingness to share family stories and memories freely. You were with us during happy, celebratory occasions and some of our most difficult moments. Your legacy is that of a great man that always helped those in need. We miss you so much! Words cannot express all that you meant to us. We are eternally grateful for all the love, support, and commitment, and for always showing up for us and the entire family. We carry on because we remember one of your favorite sayings, "Échale ganas" (give it all you got, to put effort & energy into something) which encourages us to carry on.

You leave us with all the wonderful memories, love, and tranquility. It is with much love, endearment, and respect that this special dedication is for you.

A man without any history is like a tree without roots.

MALCOLM X

TABLE OF CONTENTS

Finding
Family & Ancestors

SANTA INÉS, MICHOACÁN

The story of my maternal family has always centered around the town of Santa Inés, Michoacán, México. My early childhood memories are of traveling to visit my Aunt María, her family, and our grandfather Máximo. Traveling from the U.S. to Michoacán, México by car would take us 3-4 days, as a child, the trip seemed eternal. I was always excited to read the sign that read "Santa Inés" as we arrived in town. My aunt, María's house is the second house as you enter the town, on Avenida Fernández, the main street. It appeared that all the houses shared a street-facing wall towards the main street because, from that viewpoint, I couldn't see where the houses ended. All of the houses were painted in different bright colors. My aunt's house was painted a bright yellow and the bottom 1/3 of the wall was painted a deep red. The sidewalk in front of her house had bright yellow and red tiles set in a repetitive pattern that made them appear as if they were woven. Every morning, one of my primas (female cousins) would wash the sidewalk. It is customary for the females of the house to wash the sidewalk every morning. I didn't realize it at the time, and I don't think my cousins knew it, but now as an adult and with a greater understanding of Mexican Indigenous culture, I recognize that washing sidewalks daily is an indigenous teaching.

According to stories from the elders in the family, we were descendants of Spaniards. It was difficult for me to understand how we were only descendants of Spaniards. Although my grandfather and the majority of my family are fair-skinned, my uncle Max, my (deceased) uncle Juan and I were of a darker skin tone. My uncle Jesús recalls his grandmother, Juana, and describes her as a tall, slender woman with long dark hair, dark skin, and indigenous features. Unfortunately, the only information that the family could recall only accounted for the names of my mom's parents, grandparents, and great-grandparents.

This is the fascinating story of my maternal family and the search for our roots. With the limited information that was available, I was able to discover our deep roots in Michoacán dating back to 1650.

1

Sahara (Angelita) Barragán

At the end of the day, we can endure much
more than we think we can.
~ FRIDA KAHLO

Sahara Barragán, my grandmother, was born in El Rancho El Limon, Michoacán, on February 1, 1907, at 6:00 a.m. As per the document filed in Tingüindin, Mich. Mex. Her registration of birth indicates she was the natural daughter of Juan Barragán and Luisa Mendoza. Sahara was 1 month old when her mother, Luisa, passed away from a fever. At the time of her death, Luisa was 16 years old. The family does not know all the details, but at some point, Juan made the decision to give his daughter, Sahara, to a well-established family that did not have any children. That family (name unknown) raised her in or near Santa Inés, Mich. We believe that her new family changed her name to María de Los Angeles, Angela, or Angelita at some point. All three of these names appear in various documents including some of her children's documents. In the 1930 census, she is listed as Angelita, age 22. The information about her real birth name (Sahara) was new information to the family and was discovered in 2021 as a result of this research.

ANGELITA'S ANCESTORS

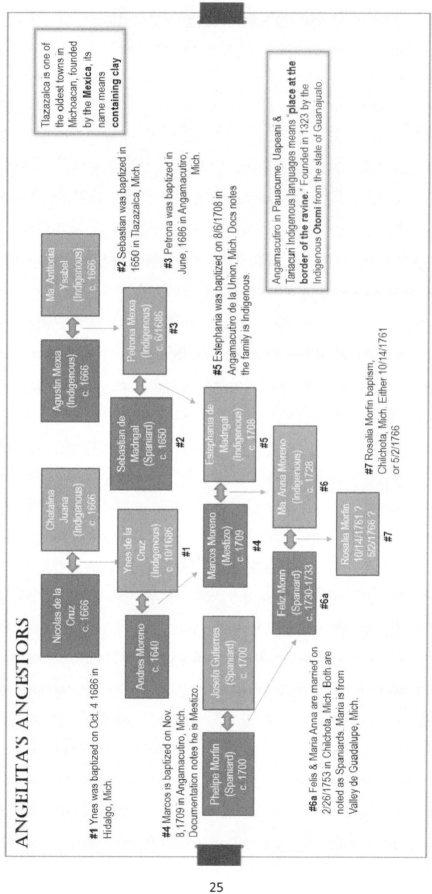

Tlazazalca is one of the oldest towns in Michoacan, founded by the **Mexica**, its name means **containing clay**

Angamacutiro in Pauacume, Uapeani & Tariacuri Indigenous languages means "**place at the border of the ravine.**" Founded in 1323 by the Indigenous **Otomi** from the state of Guanajuato

Ma. Antonia Ysabel (Indigenous) c. 1666

Agustin Mexia (Indigenous) c. 1666

Petrona Mexia (Indigenous) c. 6/1686 **#3**

Chatalina Juana (Indigenous) c. 1666

Nicolas de la Cruz c. 1666

Ynes de la Cruz (Indigenous) c. 10/1686 **#1**

Sebastian de Madrigal (Spaniard) c. 1650 **#2**

Estephania de Madrigal (Indigenous) c. 1708 **#5**

Andres Moreno c. 1640

Marcos Moreno (Mestizo) c. 1709 **#4**

Ma. Anna Moreno (Indigenous) c. 1728 **#6**

Josefa Gutierres (Spaniard) c. 1700

Feliz Morin (Spaniard) c. 1730-1733 **#6a**

Rosalia Morfin 10/14/1761 ? 5/2/1766 ? **#7**

Phelipe Morfin (Spaniard) c. 1700

#1 Ynes was baptized on Oct. 4 1686 in Hidalgo, Mich.

#2 Sebastian was baptized in 1650 in Tlazazalca, Mich.

#3 Petrona was baptized in June, 1686 in Angamacutiro, Mich.

#4 Marcos is baptized on Nov. 8, 1709 in Angamacutiro, Mich. Documentation notes he is Mestizo.

#5 Estephania was baptized on 8/6/1708 in Angamacutiro de la Union, Mich. Docs notes the family is Indigenous.

#6a Felis & Maria Anna are married on 2/26/1753 in Chilchota, Mich. Both are noted as Spaniards. Maria is from Valley de Guadalupe, Mich.

#7 Rosalia Morfin baptism, Chilchota, Mich. Either 10/14/1761 or 5/2/1766

Angelita's (Sahara's) Ancestors

#1 – Ynes de la Cruz (10th great-great-grandmother)

Ynes de la Cruz was baptized on October 4, 1686, in Hidalgo, Mich. Mex. Her documents note that the entire family is Indigenous. The document also references that the family is *"in labor"* of Salvador Gutierres in Jaquaro (now known as San Pedro Jacuaro, Mich. Mex.).

The original name of the city of Hidalgo was Taximaroa, in the P'urepécha language meaning, the altar of the gods put on the road.

#2 – Sebastían de Madrigal (10th great-great-grandfather)

Sebastían was baptized on May 1, 1650, in Tlazazalca, Mich. Mex. His documents note he is Spaniard.

Tlazazalca is one of the oldest towns in Michoacán, founded by the **Mexica**, its name means **containing clay.**

#3 – Petrona Mexica (10th great-great-grandmother)

Petrona was baptized on July 23, 1686, in Angamacutiro, Mich. México. Her documents indicate that the family is Indigenous.

Angamacutiro in Pauacume, Uapeani & Tariacuri Indigenous languages means **"place at the border of the ravine."** Founded in 1323 by the Indigenous **Otomí** from the state of Guanajuato.

#4 – Marcos Moreno (10th great-great-grandfather)

Andres Marcos was baptized on Nov. 8, 1709, in Angamacutiro, Mich. México. His documents indicate he is Mestizo and his family is from Panindicuaro, Mich. Mex. He was the legitimate son of Andres Moreno and Ynes de la Cruz.

Panindicuaro means "place of offering." Panindicuaro was a cultural border between the P'urepéchas and Chichimecas.

#5 – Estephania de Madrigal (9th great-great-grandmother)

Estephania was baptized on August 6, 1708, in Angamacutiro, Mich. México. Her documents indicate she is Indigenous and her parents are from Susupuato, Mich. México. She was the legitimate daughter of Sebastían de Madrigal & Trona Mexia. Her documents were located in a book for Indios (Indigenous), separate from records of Spaniards or non-Indigenous people.

The word Susupuato means, "place of scorpions." Susupuato consists of diverse prehispanic populations and was inhabited by groups of P'urépechas (Tarascos), Mazahuas, Otomí, and Náhuas (Mexica).

#6 – María Anna Moreno (8th great-great-grandmother)

María Anna was baptized on June 28, 1728, in Chilchota, Mich. México. Her documents indicate that her parents are Spaniards from Valle de Guadalupe, Mich., México. Her parents were Marcos Moreno & Estephania Madrigal.

#6a – María Anna Moreno & Feliz Morin (8th great-great-grandparents)

Feliz (23-25) & María Anna (25) were married on February 26, 1753, in Chilchota, Mich. México. Their documents indicate that they are both Spaniards. Feliz was originally from Valle de Camino de esta Parte (a word that was not legible) and María Anna is from Valle de Guadalupe, Mich., México.

#7 – Rosalia Morfin (7th great-great-grandmother)

Anna María Rosalia Morfin Moreno was baptized in Chilchota, Mich. México, the written document indicates she was baptized on May 2, 1766, and she originates from Guadalupe. A secondary document indicates she was baptized on October 14, 1761. Both documents indicate she is the legitimate daughter of Felis Morfin and María Anna Moreno.

ANGELITA'S ANCESTORS

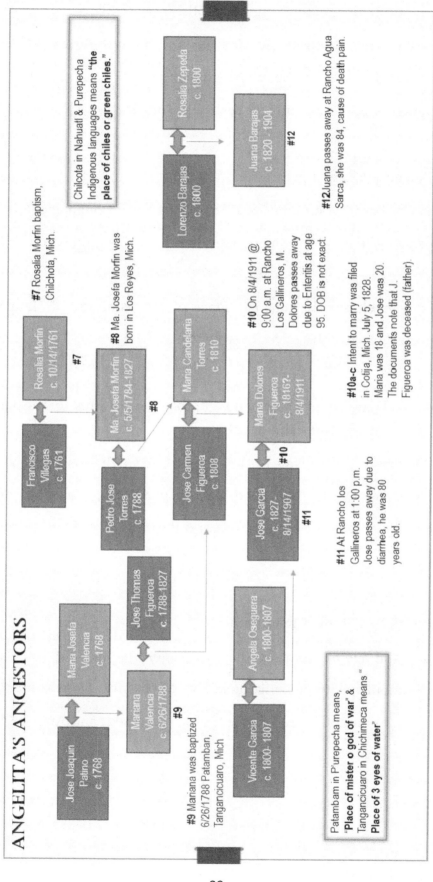

#7 Rosalia Morfin baptism, Chilchota, Mich.

Chilcota in Nahuatl & Purepecha Indigenous languages means **"the place of chiles or green chiles."**

#8 Ma. Josefa Morfin was born in Los Reyes, Mich.

#9 Mariana was baptized 6/26/1788 Patamban, Tangancicuaro, Mich

#10 On 8/4/1911 @ 9:00 a.m. at Rancho Los Gallineros, M. Dolores passes away due to Enteritis at age 95. DOB is not exact.

#10a-c Intent to marry was filed in Cotija, Mich. July 5, 1828. Maria was 18 and Jose was 20. The documents note that J. Figueroa was deceased (father).

#11 At Rancho los Gallineros at 1:00 p.m. Jose passes away due to diarrhea, he was 80 years old.

#12 Juana passes away at Rancho Agua Sarca, she was 84, cause of death pain.

Patambam in P'urepecha means, **"Place of mister o god of war"** & Tangancicuaro in Chichimeca means " **Place of 3 eyes of water"**

#8 María Josefa Morfin (6ᵗʰ great-great-grandmother)

María Josefa was baptized on May 5, 1784, in Los Reyes, Mich., Mex. Her documents indicate that she was Spaniard from Ziquitaro, Mich. México. She was the legitimate daughter of Francisco Villegas & Rosalia Morfin.

#9 – Maríana Balencia (6ᵗʰ great-great-grandmother)

Maríana was baptized on June 26, 1788, in Patamban, Tangancicuaro, Mich., Mex. Her documents note she is the legitimate daughter of Jose Joaquin Patiño & María Josefa Balencia.

Patambam in P'urépecha means, "Place of the bamboos" & Tangancicuaro in Chichimeca means "Place of the 3 eyes of water."

#10 -María Dolores Figueroa, Jose Carmen Figueroa(4ᵗʰ great-great-grandparents) & María Torres (5ᵗʰ great-great-grandmother)

María Dolores passed away at the Ranch Los Gallineros (the roosters) in the municipality of Cotija, Mich., Mex. She was 95 years old; the cause of death was Eutheritis. She was the widow of Jose Garcia and the daughter of Jose Carmen Figueroa and María Torres.

#11 – Jose Garcia (4ᵗʰ great-great-grandfather)

Jose passed at age 80 from diarrhea on August 14, 1907, at Los Gallineros (the roosters) Ranch, municipality of Cotija de la Paz, Mich. Mex. He was married to María Dolores Figueroa, his parents were Vicente Garcia (deceased) and Angela Oseguera.

ANGELITA'S ANCESTORS

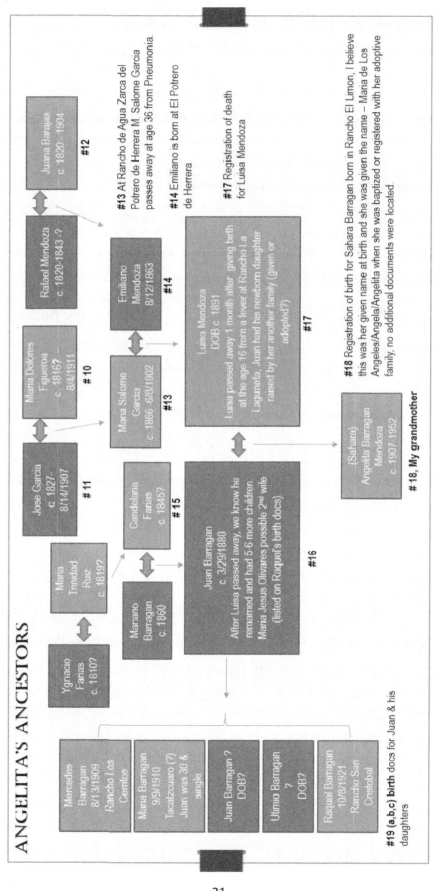

Ygnacio Farias c. 1810?

Maria Trinidad Ruiz c. 1819?

Jose Garcia c. 1827 – 8/14/1907 #11

Maria Dolores Figueroa c. 1816? – 8/4/1911 #10

Rafael Mendoza c. 1820–1843 –?

Juana Barajas c. 1820 – 1904 #12

Mariano Barragan c. 1860

Candelaria Farias c. 1845? #15

Maria Salome Garcia c. 1866 6/8/1902 #13

Emiliano Mendoza 8/12/1863 #14

Juan Barragan c. 3/29/1880

After Luisa passed away, we know he remarried and had 5-6 more children. Maria Jesus Olivares possible 2nd wife (listed on Raquel's birth docs)

#16

Luisa Mendoza DOB c. 1891

Luisa passed away 1 month after giving birth at the age 16 from a fever at Rancho La Laguneta. Juan had his newborn daughter raised by her another family (given or adopted?)

#17

(Sahara) Angelita Barragan Mendoza c. 1907-1952

 # 18, My grandmother

#13 At Rancho de Agua Zarca del Potrero de Herrera M. Salome Garcia passes away at age 36 from Pneumonia.

#14 Emiliano is born at El Potrero de Herrera

#17 Registration of death for Luisa Mendoza

#18 Registration of birth for Sahara Barragan born in Rancho El Limon, I believe this was her given name at birth and she was given the name – Maria de Los Angeles/Angela/Angelita when she was baptized or registered with her adoptive family, no additional documents were located.

Mercedes Barragan 8/13/1909 Rancho Los Cerritos

Maria Barragan 9/9/1910 Tacatzcuaro (?) Juan was 30 & single

Juan Barragan ? DOB?

Ultimo Barragan ? DOB?

Raquel Barragan 10/8/1921 Rancho San Cristobal

#19 (a,b,c) birth docs for Juan & his daughters

#12 – Juana Barajas (4th great-great-grandmother)

Juana passes away at age 84 on January 27, 1904, at 4:00 p.m. at the Agua-Sarca Ranch. The cause of death was pain, no further explanation was given. Widow of Rafael Mendoza and daughter of Lorenzo Barajas (deceased) and Rosalia Zepeda.

13- María Salome Garcia (great-great-grandmother)

María Salome passed away at age 36 from pneumonia on June 8, 1902, at 6:00 a.m. at the Agua Santa del Potrero de Herrera Ranch. María Salome was the natural daughter of Jose Garcia and María Dolores Figueroa. She is survived by her husband Emiliano Mendoza. The witnesses to the events were Luis Gutierres and Jose Jimenez, both of age, married, and laborers.

#14 – Emiliano Mendoza (great-great-grandfather)

Emiliano was baptized on August 12, 1863, in Tingüindin, Michoacán, México. He was born at El Potrero de Herrera on August 7, 1863. His parents were Rafael Mendoza & Juana Barajas.

#15 – Candelaria Farias (great-great-grandmother)

Candelaria passed away on April 5, 1905, at 10:00 p.m. in Cotija de la Paz, Mich. Mex. She passed away at age 60 from kidney cancer & ascites diarrhea. She was the widow of Maríano Barragán and the daughter of Ignacio Farias (deceased) and Trinidad Ruiz.

#16 – Juan Barragán (great-grandfather)

Juan was baptized on March 30, 1880, in Cotija, Mich., México. He was born on March 29, 1880, and his parents were Maríano Barragán & Candelaria Farias. His godparents were Francisco & Marcelina Barragán.

17- Luisa Mendoza (great-grandmother)

Luisa passed away from a fever on March 5, 1907, at 2:00 p.m. at Rancho La Laguneta. Luisa was 16 years old, married, and had a 1-month-old daughter, Sahara Barragán (my grandmother). Her parents were Emiliano Mendoza & María Salome Garcia. This document was filed in Tacátzcuaro, Mich., México.

#18 – Sahara Barragán (Angelita) (my grandmother)

Sahara Barragán, my grandmother, was born at El Limon Ranch on February 1, 1907, at 6:00 a.m. This document was filed in Tingüindin, Mich. Mex. And it indicates she is the natural daughter of Juan Barragán and Luisa Mendoza. Sahara was 1 month old when her mother (#17 Luisa Mendoza) passed away. Juan made the decision to give Sahara to a well-established family that did not have any children. This part of her life story is well-known in the family. We believe that the family that raised her changed her name to María de Los Angeles, Angela, or Angelita, however, no documents regarding changes to her name were located.

#19 –Juan Barrangan's other daughters

Juan Barragán had several daughters after Sahara. Mercedes Barragán was born in 1909, María Barragán in 1910 and Raquel Barragán in 1921. The family also believed he had 2 sons, Juan Barragán and Utimio Barragán however no documents were located regarding them. The documents for Mercedes and María indicate that Juan presented both of them as his daughters. The documents do not identify the mothers. Raquel's documents indicate that she is the natural daughter of Juan Barragán and María Jesús Olivares, commonly known as "Jesúsita."

2

Macimo Fernández

I sustain myself with the love of family
~ MAYA ANGELOU

Macimo Fernández Barragán, my grandfather, was born at 3:00 p.m. on March 4, 1901, in Santa Inés, Michoacán. His birth was recorded at the Villa de Tingüindin, Michoacán on March 30, 1901. The document states that Victoriano Fernández, a neighbor from Santa Inés, presented himself to give the notice of birth. Victoriano presented a registration from the town of Tacátzcuaro, Mich. He declared that at 3:00 p.m. on March 4, 1901, a male child was born alive and given the name Macimo Fernández Barragán. Macimo, was the natural child of Victoriano Fernández & Juana Barragán. Witnesses to the events were two citizens Antonio & Miguel Fernández, of age, married, laborers, and living in the same town.

My grandfather Macimo had an older brother, Cesario Fernández Barragán (born 1899), a younger brother, German Fernández Barragán (born 1905), and twin sisters, María Refugio y Exiquia Fernández Barragán (born 1910). His sister Exiquia passed away at 3 months old due to whooping cough.

MAXIMO'S ANCESTORS

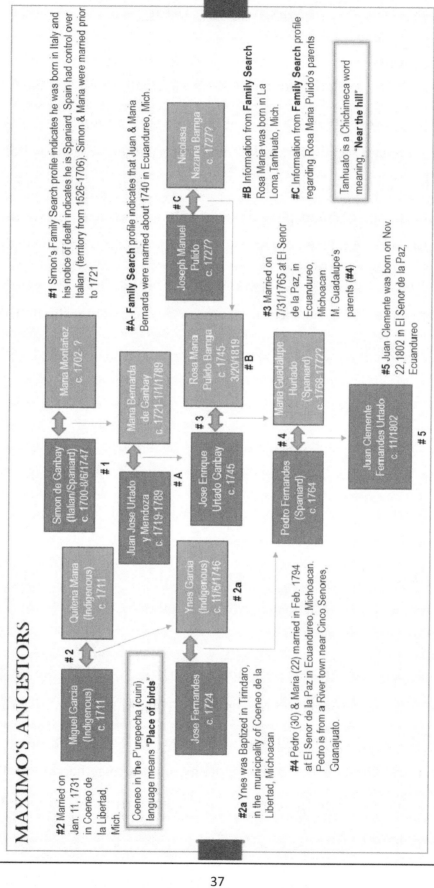

#1 Simon's Family Search profile indicates he was born in Italy and his notice of death indicates he is Spaniard. Spain had control over Italian (territory from 1526-1706). Simon & Maria were married prior to 1721

#A- Family Search profile indicates that Juan & Maria Bernarda were married about 1740 in Ecuandureo, Mich.

#B Information from **Family Search** profile Rosa Maria was born in La Loma, Tanhuato, Mich.

#C Information from **Family Search** profile regarding Rosa Maria Pulido's parents

Tanhuato is a Chichimeca word meaning, **"Near the hill"**

#3 Married on 7/31/1765 at El Senor de la Paz, in Ecuandureo, Michoacan M. Guadalupe's parents **(#4)**

#5 Juan Clemente was born on Nov. 22,1802 in El Senor de la Paz, Ecuandureo

#2 Married on Jan. 11, 1731 in Coeneo de la Libertad, Mich.

Coeneo in the Purepecha (cuini) language means **"Place of birds"**

#2a Ynes was Baptized in Tirindaro, in the municipality of Coeneo de la Libertad, Michoacan

#4 Pedro (30) & Maria (22) married in Feb. 1794 at El Senor de la Paz in Ecuandureo, Michoacan. Pedro is from a River town near Cinco Senores, Guanajuato.

Simon de Garibay (Italian/Spaniard) c. 1700-8/6/1747

Maria Montañez c. 1702-?

Juan Jose Urtado y Mendoza c. 1719-1789

Maria Bernarda de Garibay c. 1721-1/1/1789

Jose Enrique Urtado Garibay c. 1745

Rosa Maria Pulido Barriga c. 1745 3/20/1819

Joseph Manuel Pulido c. 1727?

Nicolasa Nazaria Barriga c. 1727?

Miguel Garcia (Indigenous) c. 1711

Quiteria Maria (Indigenous) c. 1711

Ynes Garcia (Indigenous) c. 11/6/1746

Jose Fernandes c. 1724

Pedro Fernandes (Spaniard) c. 1764

Maria Guadalupe Hurtado (Spaniard) c. 1768-1772?

Juan Clemente Fernandes Urtado c. 11/1802

#1 #A #3 #B #C #2 #2a #4 #5

Máximo's Ancestors

#1 – Simon De Garibay & María Montañes (8th great-great-grandparents)

The record located indicates that Simon was born in Italy in 1700. The document indicates he is Spaniard (Spain controlled the territory today known as Italy from 1526-1706). According to the records, Simon and María were married before 1721. This document indicates that Simon passed away and was buried on August 6, 1747, in Tlazazalca, Mich., Mex. Simon had "estancia" (stay) in Patzímaro, Mich. Mex. and he was married to María de Montañes, who passed away unexpectedly the cause of her death was not administered (it was not clear if this means it was not investigated, documented, or if there was no autopsy).

#2 – Miguel & Quiteria (7th great-great-grandparents)

Miguel and María Quiteria were married on January 11, 1731, in Coeneo de la Libertad, Mich., Mex. Their daughter's (María Ynes Garcia, #2a) documents indicate that they are all Indigenous from Naxanxa, today known as Naranja (orange) de Tapia, Mich., Mex.

Naxanxa was conquered by the first P'urépechas converting it at that time as part of the first settlement of the Michoaque/Michoacán P'urépecha empire.

#2a – María Ynes Garcia (6th great-great-grandmother)

María Ynes was baptized on November 6, 1746, in the town of Tiríndaro. In the municipality of Coeneo de la Libertad, Mich. Mex. She was the legitimate daughter of Miguel Garcia and Quiteria María. Her documents indicate that María Ynes and her entire family including her godparents are all Indigenous from Naxanxa today known as Naranja de Tapia, Mich., Mex.

Meaning the family was in Naxanxa (original Indigenous name) prior to the town name being changed to the Spanish version of Naranja.

#3- Jose Enrique Hurtado & Rosa María Pulido (6th great-great-grandparents)

Enrrique Hurtado married RosaMaría Pulido on July 31, 1765, at the El Señor de la Paz Parrish in Ecuandureo, Mich., Mex. The archives indicate that RosaMaría was born in La Loma, Tanhuato, Mich., Mex. The enclosed document indicates that María Pulido was Spaniard and she passed away on March 20, 1819.

Ecuandureo is a Chichimeca word meaning, **"place where they sell coal."**

#4- María Guadalupe Hurtado & Pedro Fernándes (5th great-great-grandparents)

On February 7, 1794, in Ecuandareo, Mich. An intent to marry was filed by Pedro Fernándes, Spaniard, 30 years old and originally from Pueblo Cinco Señores, Guanajuato. He was the legitimate son of Jose Fernándes & Ynes Garcia, both deceased. The intent to marry declares that he wishes to enter into matrimony with María Guadalupe Hurtado. That they are not related and that he is a person without any commitments to another. The church representative explained the seriousness of marriage and his obligation under the holy cross. The document notes Pedro does not know how to write, so the church representative signed on his behalf.

That same day, María Guadalupe Hurtado, Spaniard, doncella (virgin) of 22 years of age, from Patzímaro de Avina, Mich. presented herself declaring she wanted to enter into matrimony with Pedro Fernándes. María Guadalupe was the legitimate daughter of Jose Enrrique Hurtado & Rosa María Pullido, both living. She declared that she and Pedro are not related.

On February 24, 1794, Pedro Fernándes and María Guadalupe Hurtado are married.

#5- Juan Clemente Fernándes Urtado (4th great-great-grandfather)

Juan Clemente was born on October 25, 1802. He was baptized on November 22, 1802, in Ecuandureo, Mich. His documents indicate that he is a Spaniard child 28 days old. He was the legitimate son of Pedro Fernándes & María Guadalupe Urtado from Patzímaro. His godparents were Jose Franco Urtado & his mother Ma. Guadalupe Urtado, Spaniards.

MAXIMO'S ANCESTORS

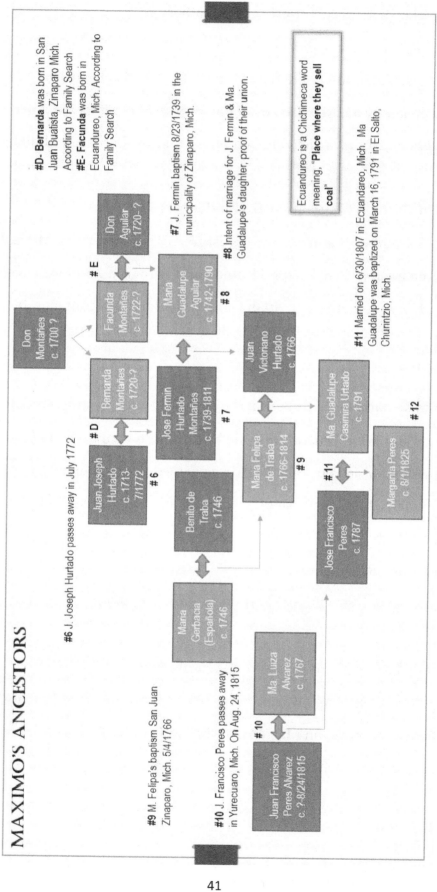

#D- **Bernarda** was born in San Juan Buatista, Zinaparo Mich. According to Family Search

#E- **Facunda** was born in Ecuandureo, Mich. According to Family Search

#7 J. Fermin baptism 8/23/1739 in the municipality of Zinaparo, Mich.

#8 Intent of marriage for J. Fermin & Ma. Guadalupe's daughter, proof of their union.

#11 Married on 6/30/1807 in Ecuandareo, Mich. Ma Guadalupe was baptized on March 16, 1791 in El Salto, Churintzio, Mich.

Ecuandureo is a Chichimeca word meaning, "**Place where they sell coal**"

#6 J. Joseph Hurtado passes away in July 1772

#9 M. Felipa's baptism San Juan Zinaparo, Mich. 5/4/1766

#10 J. Francisco Peres passes away in Yurecuaro, Mich. On Aug. 24, 1815

Don Montañes c. 1700-?

Don Aguilar c. 1720-?

Facunda Montañes c. 1722-? # E

Maria Guadalupe Aguilar c. 1742-1790 # 8

Bernarda Montañes c. 1720-? # D

Jose Fermin Hurtado Montañes c. 1739-1811 # 7

Juan Victoriano Hurtado c. 1766

Juan Joseph Hurtado c. 1713 7/1772 # 6

Maria Felipa de Traba c. 1766-1814 # 9

Ma. Guadalupe Casimira Urtado c. 1791

Benito de Traba c. 1746

Jose Francisco Peres c. 1787

Margarita Peres c. 8/1/1825 # 12

Maria Gertacia (Española) c. 1746

Ma. Luiza Alvarez c. 1767

Juan Francisco Peres Alvarez c. ?-8/24/1815 # 10

11

#6- Juan Joseph Hurtado (8th great-great-grandfather)

Juan Joseph was baptized on October 3, 1713, in Tlazazalca, Mich. Mex. His parents were Ignacio Urtado & Francisca Yepes. His baptism registration indicates that he and his entire family are Mestizos from the town of Huapamacato, Mich, Mex. In July 1772, Juan Joseph passes away leaving behind his widow, Bernarda Montañes.

#7- Jose Fermin Hurtado (7th great-great-grandfather)

Joseph Fermin was baptized on August 23, 1739, in Zináparo, Mich., Mex. He was the legitimate son of Juan Joseph Hurtado and Bernarda Montañes from the town of Tarímbaro. His godparents were Juan Garibay & Manuela Montañes, his uncle and áunt.

#8- Jose Fermin & María Guadalupe Aguilar (7th great-great-grandparents)

On May 30, 1789 in Ecuandureo, Mich., Mex. Jose Fermin & María Guadalupe Urtado's daughter, María Petronilla Urtado, is named in this intent to marry. María Petronilla will marry Jose María Sandoval, Spaniard, 18 years old, and originally from Cerro Colorado Yurécuaro, Mich., Mex. Jose María was the legitimate son of Juan Sandoval and María Rosalia Diaz.

**According to research, José Fermin & Maria Guadalupe were first cousins. **

#9- María Phelipa de Traba (6th great-great-grandmother)

María Phelipa de Traba was born on May 1, 1766, in Santa Barbara, Mich., Mex. María Phelipa was baptized on May 4, 1766, in San Juan Bautista, Zináparo, Mich., Mex. She was the legitimate daughter of Benito de Traba & María Gerbacia Leiva, both Spaniards.

#10- Juan Francisco (6th great-great-grandfather)

Juan Franco Peres passed away and is buried on August 24, 1815, in Yurécuaro, Michoacán, Mex. Juan leaves behind his widow, María Luisa Albares.

#11- Francisco Peres & María Guadalupe (5th great-great-grandparents)

On June 30, 1807 in Ecuandureo, Mich., Mex. Francisco Peres & María Guadalupe Hurtado establish their intent to marry. The document notes that Francisco is single, 18 years old, and of "Spanish quality." Francisco is originally from Patzímaro, Mich., and is the legitimate son of Juan Francisco Peres and María Luisa Alvares, both living at the time.

María Guadalupe also presents herself to declare that she would like to enter into matrimony with Francisco Peres. The document indicates that she is 17 years old, of "Spanish quality," doncella (virgin) and she is the legitimate daughter of Juan Victoriano & María Felipa Trava, both living at the time.

#12- Margarita Peres & Juan Fernández (4th great-great-grandparents)

On March 28, 1843, Juan Fernándes & Margarita Peres marry. Juan is originally from Patzímaro, Mich., Spaniard and 38 years old. He is the legitimate son of Pedro Fernándes (deceased) & Guadalupe Hurtado. Margarita Peres, is originally from Patzímaro, Mich., Spaniard, and she is 15 years old, she was the legitimate daughter of Franco Peres & Guadalupe Urtado (deceased). The document also indicates that Juan & Margarita were living together.

MAXIMO'S ANCESTORS

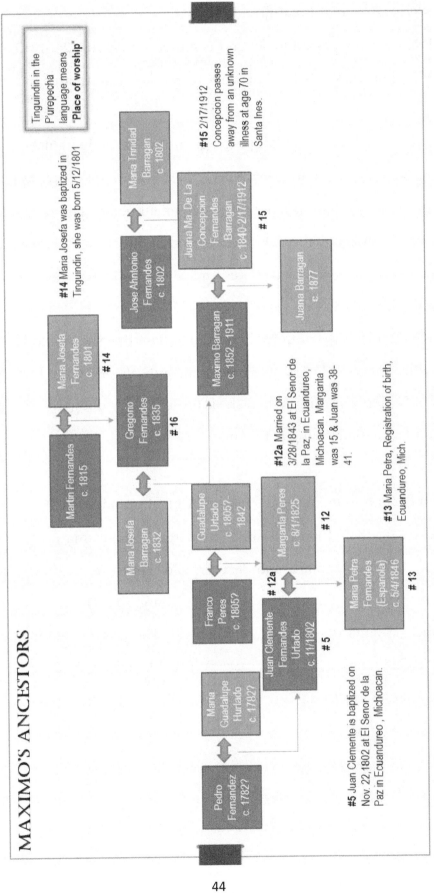

Tinguindin in the P'urepecha language means **"Place of worship"**

Pedro Fernandez c. 1782?

Maria Guadalupe Hurtado c. 1782?

Juan Clemente Fernandes Urtado c. 11/1802 — #5

Franco Peres c. 1805?

Maria Petra Fernandes (Espanola) c. 5/4/1846 — #13

Margarita Peres c. 8/1/1825 — #12a #12

Guadalupe Urtado c. 1805?-1842

Maria Josefa Barragan c. 1832

Martin Fernandes c. 1815

Gregorio Fernandes c. 1835 — #16

Maria Josefa Fernandes c. 1801 — #14

Maximo Barragan c. 1852 - 1911

Jose Antonio Fernandes c. 1802

Maria Trinidad Barragan c. 1802

Juana Ma. De La Concepcion Fernandes Barragan c. 1840- 2/17/1912 — #15

Juana Barragan c. 1877

#5 Juan Clemente is baptized on Nov. 22,1802 at El Senor de la Paz in Ecuandureo, Michoacan.

#12a Married on 3/28/1843 at El Senor de la Paz, in Ecuandureo, Michoacan. Margarita was 15 & Juan was 38-41.

#13 Maria Petra, Registration of birth, Ecuandureo, Mich.

#14 Maria Josefa was baptized in Tinguindin, she was born 5/12/1801

#15 2/17/1912 Concepcion passes away from an unknown illness at age 70 in Santa Ines.

44

#13 - María Petra (great-great-grandmother)

María Petra was born on April 29, 1846, in Patzímaro, Mich. She was baptized on May 4, 1846, in Ecuandureo, Mich. Her documents indicate she is Spaniard and was the legitimate daughter of Juan Fernándes & Margarita Peres.

#14- María Josefa (5th great-great-grandmother)

María Josefa Fecunda was born on May 12, 1801, in Santa Inés, Mich., Mex. She was baptized on May 17, 1801, at the Asuncion of María, Tingüindin, Mich. Her documents indicate she is a Spaniard and the legitimate daughter of Jose Ygnacio Fernández and María Guadalupe Espinoza.

#15- Juana María de la Concepcion Fernández (great-great-grandmother)

Juana María de la Concepcion was born on November 30, 1840, in Santa Inés, Mich. She was baptized on December 3, 1840, in Tingüindin, Mich. Her documents indicate she is of Spanish descent and was the legitimate daughter of Jose Antonio Fernándes & María Trinidad Barragán.

On February 15, 1912, at 10:00 p.m., she passed away from an unknown illness in Santa Inés, Mich. Juana was 70 years old and she was the widow of Mascimo Barragán. At the time of her passing, both her parents Antonio Fernández and María Trinidad Barragán were deceased.

#16-Jose Gregorio (Máximo Barragan's father & 4th great-great-grandfather)

Jose Gregorio Fernándes Maximo was born on March 8, 1835, in Santa Inés, Mich. He was baptized on March 16, 1835, in Tingüindin, Mich. He was the legitimate son of Martin Fernándes & María Josefa Fernándes. His godparents were Jose Anthonio Fernándes & his wife, María Fernanda Barragán from Santa Inés, Mich.

MAXIMO'S ANCESTORS

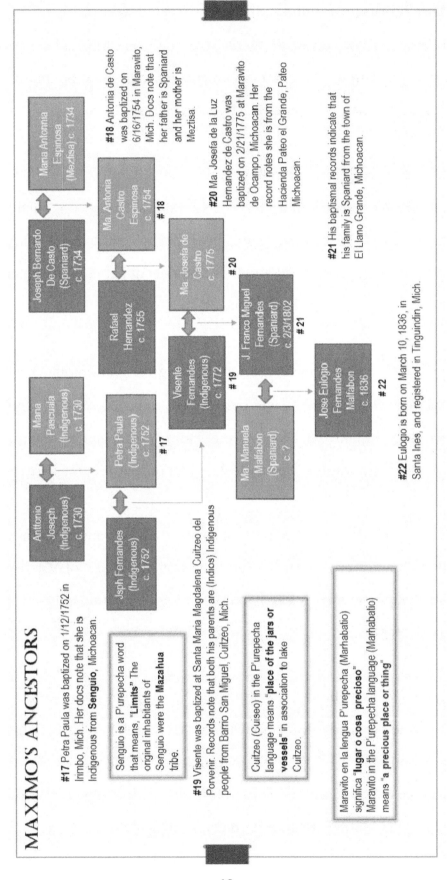

Maria Antonia Espinosa (Meztisa) c. 1734

Joseph Bernardo De Casto (Spaniard) c. 1734

Maria Pascuala (Indigenous) c. 1730

Anttonio Joseph (Indigenous) c. 1730

Ma Antonia Castro Espinosa c. 1754 #18

Rafael Hernandez c. 1755

Petra Paula (Indigenous) c. 1752 #17

Jsph Fernandes (Indigenous) c. 1752

Ma. Josefa de Castro c. 1775 #20

Visente Fernandes (Indigenous) c. 1772 #19

J. Franco Miguel Fernandes (Spaniard) c. 2/3/1802 #21

Ma. Manuela Malfabon (Spaniard) c. ?

Jose Eulogio Fernandes Malfabon c. 1836 #22

#17 Petra Paula was baptized on 1/12/1752 in Irimbo, Mich. Her docs note that she **is** Indigenous from **Senguio**, Michoacan.

Senguio is a P'urepecha word that means, "**Limits**" The original inhabitants of Senguio were the **Mazahua** tribe.

#19 Visente was baptized at Santa Maria Magdalena Cuitzeo del Porvenir. Records note that both his parents are (Indios) Indigenous people from Barrio San Miguel, Cuitzeo, Mich.

Cuitzeo (Cuiseo) in the P'urepecha language means "**place of the jars or vessels**" in association to lake Cuitzeo.

#18 Antonia de Casto was baptized on 6/16/1754 in Maravito, Mich. Docs note that her father is Spaniard and her mother is Meztisa.

#20 Ma. Josefa de la Luz Hernandez de Castro was baptized on 2/21/1775 at Maravito de Ocampo, Michoacan. Her record notes she is from the Hacienda Pateo el Grande, Pateo Michoacan.

#21 His baptismal records indicate that his family is Spaniard from the town of El Llano Grande, Michoacan.

Maravito en la lengua P'urepecha (Marhabatio) significa "**lugar o cosa precioso**" Maravito in the P'urepecha language (Marhabatio) means "**a precious place or thing**"

#22 Eulogio is born on March 10, 1836, in Santa Ines, and registered in Tinguindin, Mich.

#17- Petra Paula (6th great-great-grandmother)

Petra Paula was baptized on January 12, 1752, in Irimbo, Mich. Originally from the town of Senguio, Mich. She was the legitimate daughter of Antonio Joseph & María Pascuala, all Indigenous. Her godparents were Don Marcos Joseph de Escalante & Eventa (?).

Senguio is a P'urépecha word that means, "**limits**." The original tribes of Senguio were the Mazahuas, inside the limits of the P'urépecha border with the Mexica empire, within the Chichimeca region.

#18- María Anttonia (6th great-great-grandmother)

María Anttonia Casto Espinosa was baptized on January 16, 1754, in Maravito, Mich. Her documents indicate she was the legitimate daughter of Joseph Bernardo Garsia (Spaniard) & María Anttonia Espinosa (Mestiza) from Maravito. Her godfather was Nicolas Garsia, Spaniard, single from Maravito, Mich.

The word Maravito is derived from the P'urépecha word, Muruati, which means "**precious place or flowery place**." Maravito is known for its green landscapes The tribes that inhabited Maravito included: Matlatzincas, Otomí, Mazahuas & P'urépecha.

#19- Visente Fernández (5th great-great-grandfather)

Eugenio Vicente Fernández was born on December 16, 1772, in the San Miguel neighborhood of the town of Cuitzeo, Mich. He was baptized on December 23, 1772. His documents indicate that he was the legitimate son of Joseph Fernández & Petra Paula, all Indigenous from the San Miguel neighborhood in Cuitzeo, Mich.

Cuitzeo (Cuiseo) in the P'urépecha language means "**place of the jars or vessels**" in association to lake Cuitzeo.

#20- María Josefa de Castro (5th great-great-grandmother)

María Josefa Dela Luz Hernandez de Castro was baptized on February 21, 1775, in Maravito de Ocampo, Mich. Her documents indicate she is Spaniard from the Hacienda Pateo El Grande. She was the legitimate daughter of Rafael Hernandez & Antonia de Castro. Her godparents were Pedro Joseph Rebollar & Antonia Gertrudis de Castro from a different hacienda.

#21- Jose Franco (4th great-great-grandfather)

Jose Franco Miguel Fernández was baptized on February 3, 1802, in Morelos, Mich. His documents indicate that he is Spaniard from Llano Grande. He was the son of Visente Fernándes & María Josefa de Castro. His godparents were Pedro Joseph Hernandez & Juana Manuela, his woman.

#22- Eulogio Fernández (great-great-grandfather)

Jose Eulogio Fernándes Malfabon was born on March 10, 1836, in Santa Inés, Mich. He was baptized on March 12, 1836, in Tingüindin, Mich. He was the legitimate son of Franco Fernándes & María Manuela Malfabon from Santa Inés, Mich. His godparents were Vicente Espinosa & his mother María Maldonado from La Laguneta, Mich.

#22a- Eulogio & María Antonia Padilla (first wife)

On December 15, 1860, María Antonia Padilla passes away at the age of 40 due to inflammation in Zamora, Mich. leaving Eulogio Fernández a widower.

MAXIMO'S ANCESTORS

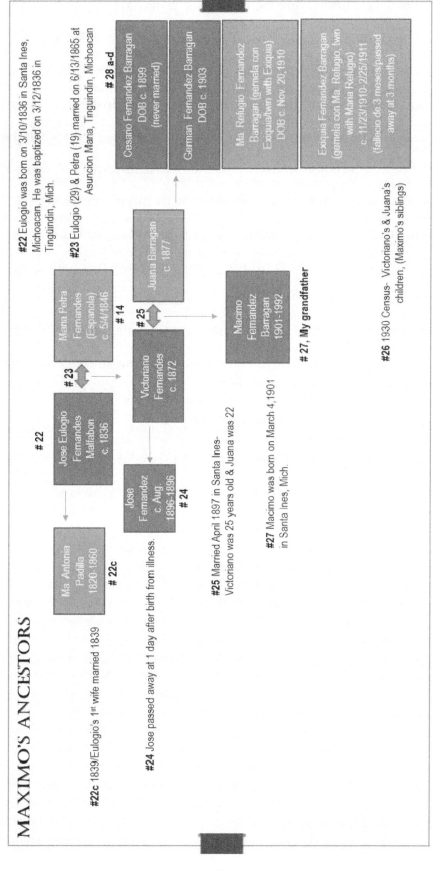

#22

#22c 1839/Eulogio's 1st wife married 1839

22c
Ma. Antonia Padilla
1820-1860

Jose Eulogio Fernandes Malfabon
c. 1836

23

Maria Petra Fernandes (Espanola)
c. 5/4/1846

14

Juana Barragan
c. 1877

25

Victoriano Fernandes
c. 1872

Jose Fernandez
c. Aug. 1896-1896

24

#24 Jose passed away at 1 day after birth from illness.

#25 Married April 1897 in Santa Ines- Victoriano was 25 years old & Juana was 22

Macimo Fernandez Barragan
1901-1992

27, My grandfather

#27 Macimo was born on March 4, 1901 in Santa Ines, Mich.

#22 Eulogio was born on 3/10/1836 in Santa Ines, Michoacan. He was baptized on 3/12/1836 in Tinguindin, Mich.

#23 Eulogio (29) & Petra (19) married on 6/13/1865 at Asuncion Maria, Tinguindin, Michoacan

28 a-d

Cesario Fernandez Barragan
DOB c. 1899
(never married)

German Fernandez Barragan
DOB c. 1903

Ma. Refugio Fernandez Barragan (gemela con Exiquia/twin with Exiquia)
DOB c. Nov 20,1910

Exiquia Fernandez Barragan (gemela con Ma. Refugio, twin with Maria Refugio)
c. 11/23/1910-2/25/1911
(fallecio de 3 meses/passed away at 3 months)

#26 1930 Census- Victoriano's & Juana's children, (Macimo's siblings)

#23- Eulogio & Petra Fernández (great-great-grandparents)

Eulogio Fernández & María Petra Fernández were married on June 13, 1865, in Tingüindin, Mich. The document indicates that they are both from Santa Inés, Mich.

Family story/verbal history, Eulogio was a teacher by profession. He supported the belief that there should be an even distribution of land for those who work the land. These beliefs were the foundation of what later became the Agrarianism movement in México. His support of those beliefs-initiated difficulties with the government and the military. The government launched a manhunt for Eulogio, and while he was on the run, Eulogio killed numerous soldiers, the exact numbers are not known. Eventually, the military surrounded him and shot him. They dragged his body through the streets of Santa Inés by horse and eventually hanged his body in an area outside of town known as "Los Pinos" (the pines). These events were shared by my grandfather, Máximo Fernández (regarding his grandfather, Eulogio, my great-great-grandfather).

The Agrarianism movement in México played a significant role before, during, and after the Mexican Revolution, as a political and social movement that demanded equitable and fair distribution of land, for those that worked the land.

#24- Jose Fernández (Victoriano's first son)

On August 6, 1896, Victoriano Fernández presented himself to the court of Tingüindin, Mich. To give notice that Jose Fernández, the son of Victoriano Fernández & Carlotta Fernández from the ranch of Santa Inés, passed away 1 day after birth from an unknown illness. Witnesses to the account were Marcelino Lazaro & Odon Fernández.

#25 Victoriano & Juana (great-grandparents)

In Tacátzcuaro, Mich., on April 3, 1897, Victoriano Fernández, 25 years of age presented himself to declare his desire to enter into marriage with Juana Barragán from the ranch of Santa Inés, Mich. Victoriano was the legitimate son of Eulogio Fernández & Petra Fernández. Swearing in the name of our Lord and the holy cross that he has no pending commitments with any other person.

That same day, Juana Barragán presented herself to declare that she effectively wants to enter into marriage with Victoriano Fernández. Swearing in the name of our Lord and the holy cross that she has no pending commitments with any other person. She originates from the ranch of Santa Inés, Mich., she is 22 years of age and is the legitimate daughter of Máximo Barragán (deceased) and Concepcion Fernández (living).

Later Concepcion Fernández presented herself and declared that she gives permission for Juana to marry Victoriano.

On May 25, 1897 in Zamora, Mich. Victoriano Fernández & Juana Barragán marry.

#26 - 1930 Census Victoriano & Juana's family

Victoriano & Juana are registered in the 1930 Census as living together in Santa Inés, Michoacán with two of their five children.

Line 70 the entry for Victoriano, single, head of household, age 60, he knows how to read and write, his profession is listed as a laborer, born in Santa Inés, Mexican citizenship, he speaks Spanish, he owns the property and his family lives in the home on his property, his religion is Catholic.

Line 71 is the entry for Juana (last name by mistake listed as Hernandez), age 58, single, knows how to read, her profession is listed as domestic, born in Santa Inés, Mexican citizenship, she speaks Spanish, and her religion is listed as Catholic.

Line 72 is the entry for Sesario, male, age 30, he knows how to read, his profession is listed as a laborer, born in Santa Inés, Mexican citizenship, he speaks Spanish, and his religion is listed as Catholic.

Line 73 is the entry for María Refugio, female, age 27, single, she knows how to read, her profession is listed as domestic, born in Santa Inés, Mexican citizenship, she speaks Spanish, and her religion is listed as Catholic.

Victoriano & Juana had 5 children, Cesario, Macimo, German, María Refugio & Exiquia (twins). The only document located for Cesario is the 1930 Census.

#27-Macimo Fernández (My grandfather)

On March 30, 1901, at the Villa de Tingüindin, Mich. Victoriano Fernández, neighbor of Santa Inés, presented himself to give notice of a birth. He declared that at 3:00 p.m. on March 4, 1901, a male child was born alive and given the name Macimo Fernández. Macimo was the natural child of Victoriano Fernández & Juana Barragán. Witnesses to the events are two citizens Antonio & Miguel Fernández, of age, married, laborers, and living in the same town.

#28a - German Fernández (Great-uncle)

The documents indicate that on June 6, 1903, in Tingüindin, Mich. A notice was received from Tacátzcuaro, Mich. Dated June 2, 1903, stating that on June 1, 1903, a male boy was born in Santa Inés, given the name German Fernández, son of Victoriano Fernández, age 35, single, laborer. Witness to the notice were Refugio Gonzalez & Porfirio Canales, of age, single, laborers, of said neighborhood.

#28b María Refugio Fernández (Great-aunt)

In the Villa of Tingüindin, Mich. On November 21, 1910, Victoriano, age 40, a single, laborer from Santa Inés, presented a birth registration from the judge in Tacátzcuaro, Mich. The registration notes that on November 20, at midnight, one female child was born alive and given the name María Refugio Fernández. She was the daughter of Victoriano. Witness to the events were 2 men, Mr. Juarez & Mr. Oseguera, of age, married, laborers, from the same town and without kinship. The document does not mention that María Refugio has a twin, Exiquia.

#28c Exiquia Fernández (Great-aunt)

In the Villa of Tingüindin, Mich. On November 24, 1910, Victoriano, age 40, a single, laborer from Santa Inés, presented a birth registration from the judge in Tacátzcuaro, Mich. The registration notes that on November 23, at 8:00 p.m., one female child was born alive and given the name Exiquia Fernández. She was the daughter of Victoriano. Witness to the events were 2 men, Rafael Cararez y Antonio Andrade, of age, married, laborers, from the same town and without kinship.

#28d Exiquia Fernández (notice of death)

In the Villa of Tingüindin, Mich. On February 25, 1911, Victoriano Fernández from Santa Inés, presented a document from the Judge in Tacátzcuaro, Mich. The document confirms that on February 24, at 10:00 a.m., Exiquia Fernández, passed away from whooping cough at three months old. She was the daughter of Victoriano Fernández and Juana Barragán. Witnesses to the events were Clemente Arteaga & Cerilo Espinosa, both of age, married, laborers, from the same town, and without kinship.

3

Máximo & Angelita Fernández

In every conceivable manner, the family is link to our past,
bridge to our future
~ ALEX HALEY

My grandparents, Máximo and Angelita, were married by the church, but no documents were located. The only paperwork that documents their union is the 1930 census, the birth registrations of their daughter, María (#5), and their son, Jesús (#9). My grandmother, Angelita, passed away in 1952, months after her son, Juan was killed in a shootout. At the time, she was approximately 45 years old and pregnant with twins. There are no pictures of her. My grandfather Maximo was approximately 5'5-5'7', slender with green eyes. After my grandmother passed away, he never remarried, he dedicated himself to his children and passed away in 1992 at the age of 92.

Of their 13 children, only 6 survived to adulthood to have families of their own.

Máximo & Angelita (Sahara) Fernández

Máximo & Angelita 1930 Census record

In the 1930 Census of Michoacán, Máximo and Angelita are recorded living together in Agua Zarca, in the municipality of Tocumbo, Michoacán, with two of their sons.

Line 47 of the census lists Máximo, married by the church, head of household, age 30, unable to read and write, an agricultural laborer by profession, born in Michoacán, Mexican citizenship, speaks Spanish and his religion is catholic.

Line 48 of the census lists Angelita, age 22, married by the church, unable to read or write, domestic, born in Michoacán, Mexican citizenship, speaks Spanish, and her religion is catholic.

Line 49 lists Juan Fernández, male, age 4, born in Michoacán, Mexican citizenship and his religion is catholic.

Line 50 lists Cesario Fernández, male, age 3, born in Michoacán, Mexican citizenship and his religion is catholic.

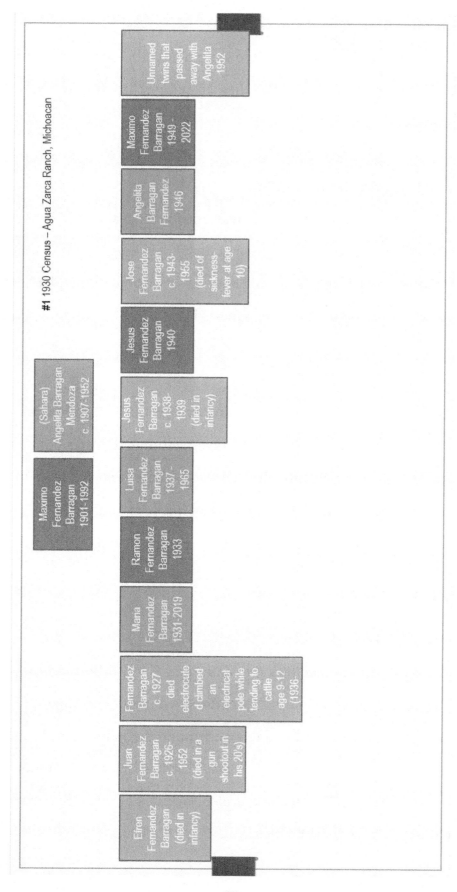

#1 1930 Census – Agua Zarca Ranch, Michoacan

#1 – Efren Fernández Barragán (my uncle)

Efren was their first-born child. There were no documents located regarding him. As per family history, we know that he died in infancy leaving Máximo & Angelita without children.

#2 – Juan Fernández Barragán (my uncle)

Juan was their second-born son. He was born in 1926 and died in April 1952. He was in his mid-20s when he died. The cause of death was by gunshot wound as a result of a shootout with another man (also from Santa Inés) near the plaza of Santa Inés, Mich. This event was witnessed by my relatives (uncles Ramon & Jesús and my aunt Maria).

#3 – Cesario Fernández Barragán, (my uncle)

Cesario was their third son. He was born in 1927. He died as a result of electrocution. He was approximately 9-12 years old, tending to cattle, and climbed up an electrical pole. He, unfortunately, got too close to the wires and the force of the current threw him to the ground. He died a few weeks later due to the burns throughout his body and his injuries. This event was witnessed by the family members including my aunt Maria.

#4 – María Fernández Barragán (my aunt)

María was Máximo & Angelita's first daughter. She was born on August 12, 1931, at 2:00 a.m. The document notes she is the legitimate daughter of Máximo Fernández & Angela Barragán. Paternal grandparents- Victoriano Fernández & Juana Barragán. Maternal grandparents- Juan Barragán & Luisa Mendoza. Her godparents were Rafael Orozco & Elenteria Orozco. The document also includes a note, "She married J. Jesús Oseguera on March 9, 1959, in Santa Inés, Mich."

#5 – Ramon Fernández Barragán (my uncle)

Ramon is Máximo & Angelita's fourth son. No documents were located.

#6 – Luisa Fernández Barragán (my aunt)

Luisa was their second daughter. She was born on May 5, 1937. No documents were located.

#7 – Jesús Fernández Barragán (my uncle)

Jesús was the fifth son. His exact date of birth is not known, the approximate year of birth was 1938, and he died in infancy. No documents were located.

#8 – Jesús Fernández Barragán (my uncle)

Jesús was the sixth son. He was born on July 20, 1940, in Periban, Michoacán. He was baptized on July 26, 1940. The document notes he is the legitimate child of Máximo Barragán and María de Los Angeles Barragán. The document also lists his paternal grandparents – Victoriano Fernández & Juana Barragán and the names of his maternal grandparents- Juan Barragán & Luisa Mendoza. His godparents were Francisco Ochoa & Ramona Higareda.

#9 – Jose Fernández Barragán (my uncle)

Jose was the seventh son. He was born approximately in 1943 (the exact date is not known) and he died in 1955. He died due to complications with his gallbladder. No documents regarding him were located.

#10 – Angelita Fernández Barragán (my mom)

Angelita was the third daughter and 10th child of the family. She was born in 1946. No documents regarding her were located.

#11 – Máximo Fernández Barragán (my uncle and godfather)

Máximo was the eighth son. He was born in 1949, in Santa Inés, Mich. No documents regarding him were located.

#12 & #13 –Fernández Barragán Twins

In May of 1952, months after Juan was killed in the shoot-out, Angelita, passed away while pregnant with twins.

Fernández Barragán Family Descendants

#1

#2

#3

#4

#5

#1-Aunt Maria's wedding portrait

#2- Aunt Maria's family photo

#3- Grandfather Maximo & his sister, (Great Aunt) Refugio, Santa Inés, Mich.

#4- Angelita (mom) & Aunt Maria, Los Reyes, Mich.

#5- Uncle Max, Mom, Uncle Jesus, Grandfather Maximo, Aunt Maria, Uncle Ramon, Uruapan, Mich. 1992

María Fernández de Oseguera & family

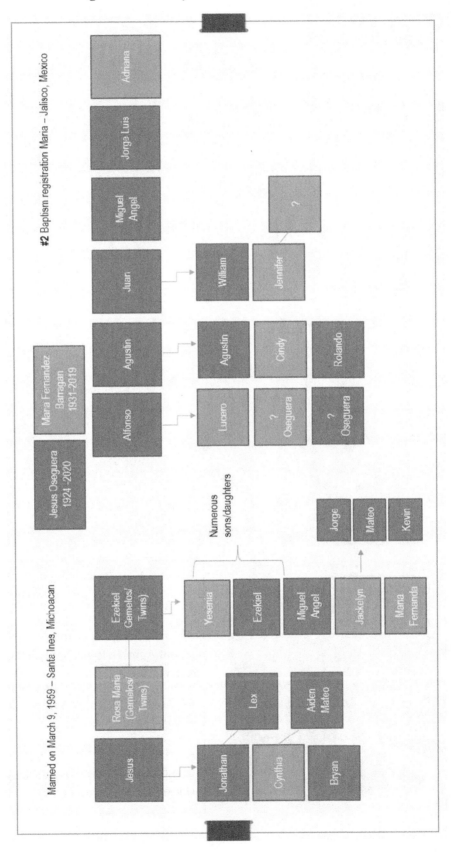

#1

#2

#3

#4

#5

#6

#1- Áunt Maria with her first-born son, Jesús

#2- The cousins in Santa Inés c. 1975- Alejandra, Jorge, Agustin, Adriana, Miguel Angel, Juan, Ezekiel, Alfonso & Jesús

#3- Aunt Maria with her husband Uncle Jesús

#4- Rosa Maria, Adriana, Aunt Maria, Ezekiel, Grandfather,& Uncle Max

#5 Aunt Maria & her son, Jorge

#6 Aunt Maria & Grandfather Maximo

Ramon Fernández & family

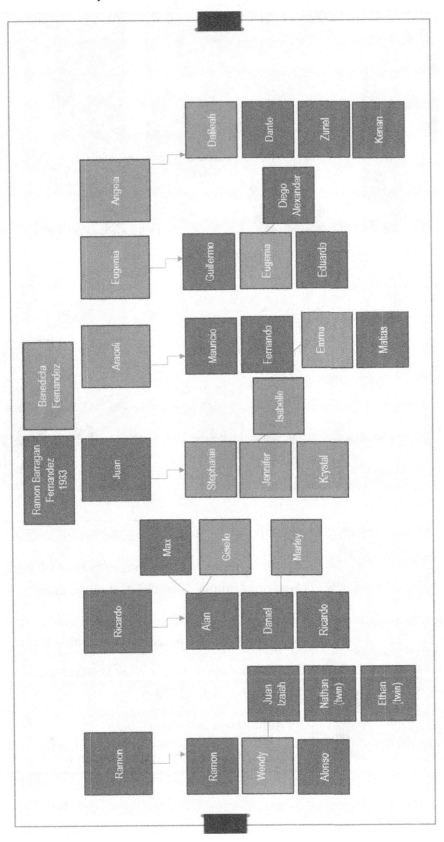

#1

#2

#3

#4

#1-Uncle Ramon at 18-20 years old

#2- The cousins Araceli, Alejandra, Eugenia & Angela- Las Lomas, Watsonville, CA c. 1975

#3-Uncle Ramon, Angelita (mom) & Uncle Max

#4- Fernández family 25th-wedding anniversary family portrait - Ricardo, Ramon Jr., Uncle Ramon, Juan, Aunt Beni, Eugenia, Araceli & Angela, Uruapan, Mich., México

#5 Nakai, Aunt Beni, Alejandra, Uncle Ramon, Kairese & Ray -Sacramento, CA

#5

Luisa Fernández Barragán & family

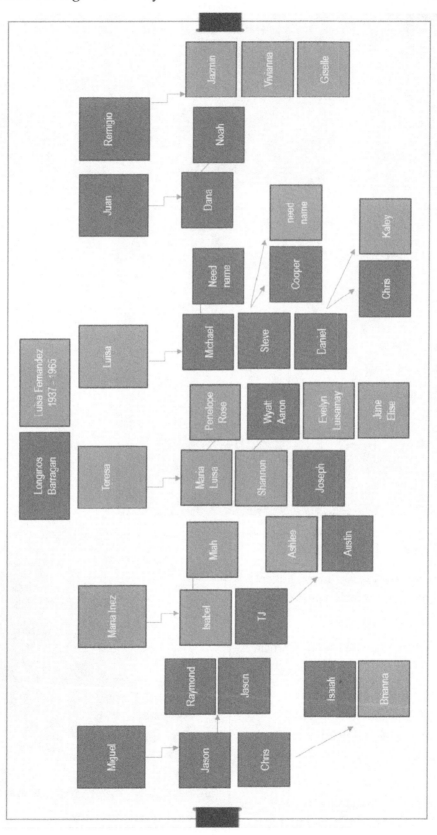

Áunt Luisa with her first-born son, Miguel
Santa Inés, Michoacán, México

Miguel, Inés y Teresa – Aunt Luisa's first 3 children

Jesús Fernández, Angelita Fernández y Máximo Fernández & their families

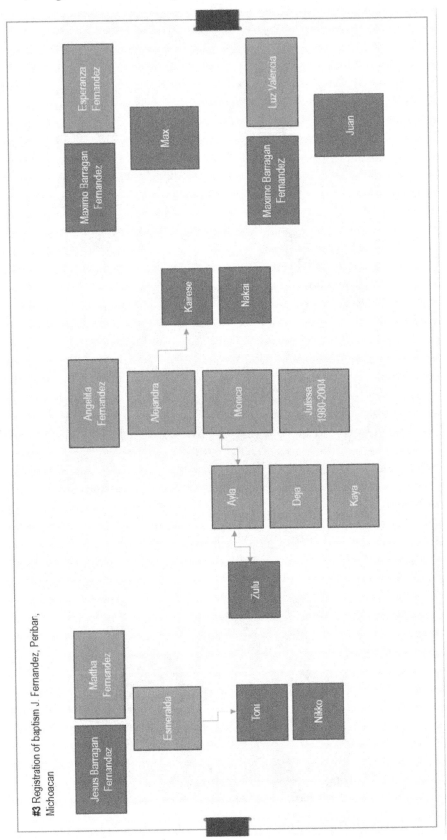

#3 Registration of baptism J. Fernández, Peribar, Michoacan

#1

#2

#3

#4

#5

#1- Uncle Jesús, 20 years old

#2- Grandfather Maximo & Uncle Jesús

#3- Uncle Jesús and his wife, Marta

#4- Uncle Jesús & his daughter Esmeralda

#5- Uncle Max, Angelita (mom), Uncle Jesús, Alejandra & Aunt Maria Morgan Hill, CA

#1

#2

#3

#1- Monica, Grandfather
Maximo & Alejandra, c.
1977/78, Watsonville, CA

#2- Baby Ayla, Monica,
Alejandra, Julissa, & Mom,
San José, CA- c. 1993/4

#3- Mom, Nakai, Zulu, Uncle
Max & Kairese, San José, CA
2018

#4- Terrence, Kairese, Nakai
& Alejandra, San José, CA,
2021

#4

#1

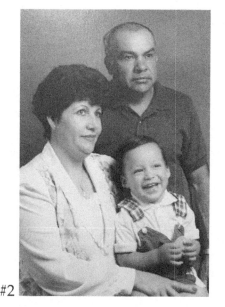

#2

#3

#4

#5

#1- Uncle Max & godmother's wedding photo with baby Alejandra, Watsonville, CA

#2-Uncle Max, Godmother & their son, Max.

#3- Grandfather & Uncle Max, making carnitas, Uruapan or Santa Inés, Mich.

#4- Aunt Maria & Uncle Max, Aunt Maria's house, Santa Inés, Michoacán

#5- Uncle Max, Juan (son) & his 2nd wife, Luz Maria

75

#1- Julissa, c. 1985, #2- Monica, Alejandra y Julissa, c. 1991/2, #3- Uncle Jesus & Mom, 2022 Watsonville, CA, #4- Kaya, Ayla, Déjá, c. 2006, #5- Ayla, Kaya, Déjá, c. 2022, #6- Nakai, Angelita (mom), Kairese, c. 2016, Carmel, CA, #7- Kairese, Mom, Nakai, 2017, San José, CA.

4

Your Story

True to your own ancestors, therefore true to yourself
~ RUSSELL MEANS

This section will offer you step-by-step instructions to help you begin to discover your family's story. I've included a template to get you started, and I have listed additional resources that have helped me in my search. Additionally, I'm including a list of terms, observations, and reoccurring themes that I've come across and that have been defined to help you move past them. Enjoy this experience, trace your roots, learn your history and know your family story. I hope this book inspires you to write a book about your family...the world needs our stories.

THE BEGINNING OF YOUR STORY

①

Complete the family chart (template) with the information that you have available. You may not have exact details or dates, but that is okay.

②

Create a free user account on one of the numerous free genealogy websites (one that I use often is www.familysearch.com)
Begin by searching for the records of your parents/grandparents.

③

I would also encourage you to take a DNA test. The information provided will help you locate the original places your ancestors descend from.

- ✓ Purchase DNA kit over the counter or online
- ✓ Submit a saliva sample by mail (instructions will be included in the kit)
- ✓ Receive your results online (email)
- ✓ Membership and additional services are **optional**

Family chart template

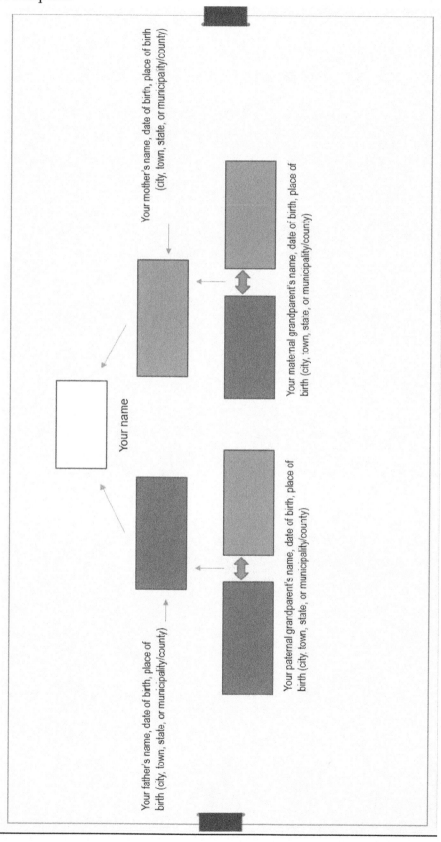

RESOURCES FROM MR. JOHN P. SCHMAL

Searching for your Indigenous Roots in México - YouTube discussion with the Los Angeles Public Library, Los Angeles, CA (lecture in English)

https://www.youtube.com/watch?v=8R3FMyzKbS0&t=9s

Mr. Schmal's website includes information on each state in México:

https://indigenousMéxico.org/

A slide from Mr. Schmal's presentation to help envision the number of great-grandparents each of us descends from.

Who am I?

Each of us has two parents, four grandparents, eight great-grandparents and 16 great-great-grandparents. Fourteen generations ago – around 1540 – you had 16,384 12th great-grandparents.

Generations Back from You	Generation No. (Starting with Your Parents)	No. of Persons in this Generation	Cumulative No. of Individuals	Approximate Year
Self	0	1	1 (You)	1960
Parents	1	2	3	1930
Grandparents	2	4	7	1910
Great-Grandparents	3	8	16	1890
2nd Great-Grandparents	4	16	31	1860
3rd Great-Grandparents	5	32	62	1830
4th Great-Grandparents	6	64	127	1800
5th Great-Grandparents	7	128	255	1770
6th Great-Grandparents	8	256	511	1740
7th Great-Grandparents	9	512	1023	1700
8th Great-Grandparents	10	1,024	2,047	1670
9th Great-Grandparents	11	2,048	4,095	1640
10th Great-Grandparents	12	4,096	8,191	1600
11th Great-Grandparents	13	8,192	16,383	1570
12th Great-Grandparents	14	16,384	32,767	1540

NATIVE MAP WHICH IDENTIFIES THE ANCESTRAL LANDS OF NATIVE PEOPLES

https://native-land.ca/

This site allows you to enter the name of a town, city, or region and the map will indicate the native peoples of that particular land.

Disclaimer: The map is not to be used as an academic or legal resource. Sourcing data on Indigenous territories is a delicate process therefore the map should be used with an understanding that areas may be incorrect according to local nations and individual interpretations. We are in a constant state of research and adjustment to the map in an effort to remain as accurate as possible, however, errors may exist. Thank you.

TERMS AND OBSERVATIONS

1. Having a first and last name is a colonizing practice. Indigenous peoples had one name and that was an acceptable custom. When the Spaniards arrived, they came across native people with one name, it was a common practice to baptize indigenous people and give them a Spanish first and last name. A common last name imposed was De La Cruz (that literally translates to, of the cross) aimed at forcing religion onto the Indigenous people.

    For example - Ynes De La Cruz, #1 on my grandmother's list.

2. **Legitimate** son/daughter refers to an individual who was born to a married couple.

3. **Natural** son/daughter refers to an individual that was born to unwed parents.

4. There are many words that are spelled in different ways, for example:

    Yndio/Indio, Balencia/Valencia, Ahntonnio/Antonio, Mexia/Mejia, Meztiso/Mestiso, etc.

5. Observation – when a person was identified as indigenous and if their tribe isn't mentioned, additional research is required to identify tribe affiliation. In order to identify the tribe, you must research the town of origin of the person, luckily there is usually a town, city, or region that is mentioned.

    For example, #5 on my grandmother's list, Estephania de Madrigal, is identified as Indigenous from Angamacutiro, Mich. No tribe is mentioned in her documents, so I researched the town of Angamacutiro and discovered that the original inhabitants of that territory were the Otomí. It is very likely that they were in fact Otomí. This was a repetitive finding in my search.

6. The term, "al labor" – is a bit unclear, but means some type of labor arrangement, probably meaning the person in the record worked on the land of another, or it was a way of identifying that person (especially if they had a common name).

7. The names of many indigenous towns were changed over time.

For example:

Jaquaro	Jacuaro	San Pedro Jacuaro
Indigenous name	Spanish version	Religious version
Original	Transitional	Current

8. The word "finado" means deceased.

9. The word "doncella" means the woman was a virgin or pure. This term was only used to describe women identified as "Española/Spaniard," but not used for Indigenous women.

10. The word "parbulo" means a young child or infant.

11. Intent to marry is different from marriage. During the intent to marry, the groom and bride would present themselves to the church/court and declare their intentions to enter into marriage. Sometimes the parents of the bride/groom would also present themselves to state on the record that they were in agreement and gave their consent to the union.

12. There are many documents that identify a person as an "Español" (Spaniard) however, there was no indication of how that was proven. Based on research, it was very subjective, it was basically the opinion of the person recording the information. If the party was fair/light-skinned, they were considered "Español."

13. Conflicting information, often you will come across records in which a person is identified as "Español" in one document, and that same person will be identified as Indigenous or Mestizo in another document. Again, subjective.

14. In almost all of the documents that I was able to locate, the date of the document and the date of the event (birth, marriage, or death) is different. It is important to read the document in its entirety to get the full picture of the sequence of events. Factors to consider may include transportation, health, financial constraints, distance, etc.

15. A DNA admixture test reveals our ancestor's geographic origins over the last several centuries, showing us our ethnic breakdown.

16. There were a few documents that noted that the person was of "Calidad Español" which means "Spaniard quality" although I could not locate a definition for this, it is safe to say it was a desirable quality vs. being identified as Indigenous.

17. Records were kept in separate "books" by race, both jurisdictions and churches kept Indigenous records and the records of "others" separately. For example, the record for #5 on my grandmother's list, Estephania de Madrigal was located in the book of Indigenous records.

ABOUT THE AUTHOR

Alejandra is a descendant of various tribes including Chichimecas, Matlatzinca, Mexica (Nahuas), Mazahuas, Otomí, and P'urépecha. The majority of her DNA indicates that she is a descendant of the Indigenous peoples of the Southwest United States and Central México. Her admixture results also trace origins in Basque Country, Cyprus, France, Italy (northern), Northern Africa, Portugal, Senegal, and Spain. Her family tree identified individuals with origins in Spain and Italy.

She was born and raised on Ahmah (Aaa-Ma) Mutsun (Moot-sun) & Ohlone (Oh-loh-nee) territory (**Watsonville, CA**). Currently, she resides on the unceded lands of the Muwekma Ohlone (mah-WEK-mah Oh-loh-nee) and the Thamien (Thah-mee-en) Nation (**San José, CA**).

In mid-2018, Alejandra experienced what she describes as a calling from her ancestors and a spiritual awakening. She experienced a heightened sense of intuition, her waking life became more vivid, she became more connected to the natural world, and her sensitivity to physical, emotional, and energetic stimuli was amplified. Answering the calling from her ancestors, she received her indigenous name, further embraced her indigenous identity, began learning Nahuatl (the language of the Mexica) and started learning Mexica culture and teachings from elders. Guided by her ancestors, the journey has led her to research her ancestry and write this book.

Made in the USA
Middletown, DE
24 January 2024

48438935R00057